Bridgestone
BOOKS

W9-BHV-304

Earthforms

Hills

by Christine Webster

Consultant:
Robert S. Anderson, PhD
Associate Professor of Geological Sciences
University of Colorado at Boulder

Capstone *press*

Mankato, Minnesota

Bridgestone Books are published by Capstone Press,
151 Good Counsel Drive, P.O. Box 669, Mankato, Minnesota 56002.
www.capstonepress.com

Library of Congress Cataloging-in-Publication Data
Webster, Christine.
    Hills / by Christine Webster.
       p. cm.—(Bridgestone books. Earthforms)
    Includes bibliographical references and index.
    ISBN-13: 978-0-7368-3712-5 (hardcover)   ISBN-10: 0-7368-3712-4 (hardcover)
    ISBN-13: 978-0-7368-6145-8 (softcover pbk.)   ISBN-10: 0-7368-6145-9 (softcover pbk.)
    1. Mountains—Juvenile literature. I. Title. II. Series.
GB512.W435 2005
910'.914'3—dc22   2004014276

Summary: Describes hills, including how they form, plants and animals on hills, how people and
    weather change hills, hills in North America, and Silbury Hill.

Editorial Credits
Becky Viaene, editor; Juliette Peters, designer; Anne McMullen, illustrator; Wanda Winch, photo
    researcher; Scott Thoms, photo editor

Photo Credits
Corbis/Gallo Images/Martin Harvey, 12
Corel, 1
Courtesy of Dr. Kenneth F. Dewey, 16
Digital Vision /Jeremy Woodhouse, 10
Getty Images/Kirk Anderson, cover
James P. Rowan, 6, 14
Mary Evans Picture Library/Lucy Pringle, 18
Steve Mulligan, 4
Tom Till, 8

1 2 3 4 5 6 10 09 08 07 06 05

Table of Contents

What Are Hills?

Hills are raised areas of the earth's surface. They are like mountains but are much shorter. Hills are less than 1,000 feet (305 meters) tall. Some hills start as mountains. Wind and rain wear mountains down. When mountains get short enough, they are then called hills.

Hills are everywhere on earth and can be big or small. A hill can be a small mound in the backyard. People sled down large hills. Hills are even found on the ocean floor.

◀ Big hills rise above the Youghiogheny River in Pennsylvania's Ohiopyle State Park.

How Do Hills Form?

Hills are formed in many ways. Both people and nature make hills. People make hills by digging and piling soil into heaps.

Nature forms hills with wind, **glaciers**, and **landslides**. In deserts, wind blows sand off land into hills, called **sand dunes**. Dirt and rocks falling off glaciers can form hills. Piles of rock can fall or slide off valley walls. These landslides form new hills on valley floors.

◀ A trail of footprints leads to the top of a sand dune in New Mexico. Many people climb these sand dunes.

Plants on Hills

Climate affects which hills plants can grow on. The climate of India's Pachaimalai Hills is hot and rainy. People plant peanuts and sugarcane on these hills. These crops grow well in this climate.

The dry climate of Iowa's Loess Hills is good for growing grasses. These grasses include yucca, tumble grass, and clover. People plant crops, such as corn and soybeans, on these hills.

◄ Yucca plants bloom on Iowa's dry Loess Hills. People have used yucca to make rope, sandals, and soap.

Animals on Hills

Climate affects which animals live on hills throughout the world. Hills with cold climates are homes for animals with thick fur. Black bears, grizzly bears, wolves, and deer live on North American hills.

In tropical climates, elephants and wild buffalo are found on hills. India's Garo Hills make a good home for these animals.

◀ Deer have thick fur to help them stay warm in cold climates.

Weather Changes Hills

Weather often **erodes** hills. Cold weather causes water inside rocks to freeze. Frozen water can expand and break up rocks and soil.

Rain and melting snow wash broken rocks and soil down hills. Wind can also carry away **sediment**. As a hill erodes, it becomes smaller and changes shape.

◀ In Borneo, rain washes soil and trees from a hill into the river below. The hill continues to get shorter.

People Change Hills

Since hills are everywhere, people use them in many ways. Some changes to hills are easy to see. People cut trees off hills and flatten the land. They grow crops and build new roads on hills.

People also change hills in ways that are harder to see. Some people enjoy sledding and skiing down hills. People also walk and bike on hills. Over time, this causes hills to erode faster.

◀ Many people live on hills in Ecuador. People also grow bananas and coffee on some of Ecuador's hills.

Hills in North America

North America has many hills. The city of San Francisco, California, was built on hills. More than 40 hills rise as high as 376 feet (115 meters) throughout San Francisco.

The Sand Hills stretch across western Nebraska. They cover an area about the size of West Virginia. These hills were once sand dunes formed by high winds. Today, plants and grasses grow in the sandy soil.

◄ The Dismal River cuts through Nebraska's Sand Hills. Plants hold sand in place and keep it from blowing.

Silbury Hill

England's Silbury Hill is Europe's largest hill made by people. The entire hill covers more than 5 acres (2 hectares). Silbury Hill stands 130 feet (40 meters) high.

Scientists think Silbury Hill was built more than 4,600 years ago. It is made of many layers of soil. No one knows why Silbury Hill was built.

◀ Silbury Hill's flat top and perfectly round bottom are proof it was formed by people, instead of nature.

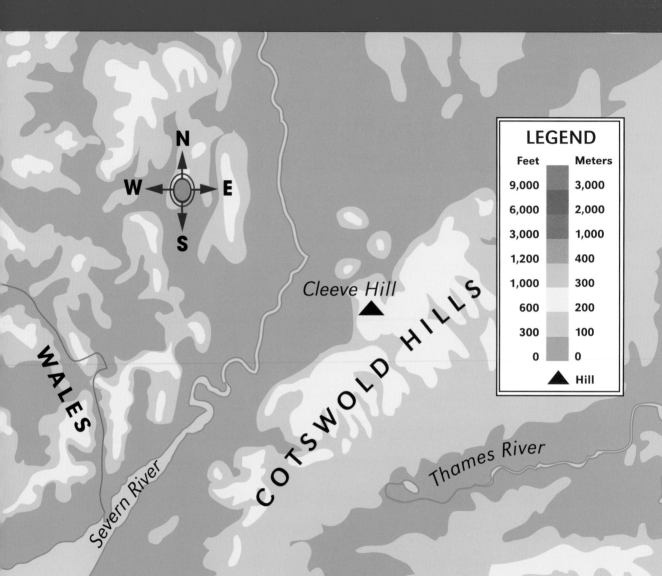

N

W ←●→ E

S

LEGEND

Feet	Meters
9,000	3,000
6,000	2,000
3,000	1,000
1,200	400
1,000	300
600	200
300	100
0	0

▲ Hill

Cleeve Hill ▲

C O T S W O L D   H I L L S

Thames River

WALES

Severn River

ENGLAND

Hills on a Map

Hills can be hard to find on maps. They may be easiest to see on **elevation** maps. On these maps, different colors show different elevations. Only large hills are labeled on maps. A triangle symbol can show a single hill or mountain.

Hills are all around us. You can probably find one near you. How is that hill used? Maybe you bike up and down the hill. Hills are used for many things. They are an important part of the land.

◀ England's Cotswold Hills and Cleeve Hill have low elevations. They are too short to be mountains.

Glossary

climate (KLYE-mit)—the usual weather in a place

elevation (el-uh-VAY-shuhn)—the height above sea level; sea level is defined as zero elevation.

erode (i-RODE)—to wear away; wind and water erode soil and rock.

glacier (GLAY-shur)—a huge moving body of ice found in mountain valleys or polar regions

landslide (LAND-slide)—a sudden slide of earth and rocks down the side of a mountain or hill

sand dune (SAND DOON)—a hill of sand made by the wind

sediment (SED-uh-muhnt)—rocks, sand, or dirt carried to a place by water, wind, or a glacier

Read More

Parks, Peggy J. *Sand Dunes.* Wonders of the World. San Diego: Kidhaven Press, 2004.

Williams, Brenda. *Hills and Mountains.* Geography Starts Here. Austin, Texas: Raintree Steck-Vaughn, 1998.

Internet Sites

FactHound offers a safe, fun way to find Internet sites related to this book. All of the sites on FactHound have been researched by our staff.

Here's how:
1. Visit *www.facthound.com*
2. Type in this special code **0736837124** for age-appropriate sites. Or enter a search word related to this book for a more general search.
3. Click on the **Fetch It** button.

FactHound will fetch the best sites for you!

Index